TAKE A CLOSER LOOK AT YOUR
Lungs

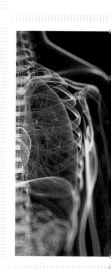

Published by The Child's World®
1980 Lookout Drive • Mankato, MN 56003-1705
800-599-READ • www.childsworld.com

Acknowledgments
The Child's World®: Mary Berendes, Publishing Director
Red Line Editorial: Editorial direction and production
The Design Lab: Design
Content Consultant: Jeffrey W. Oseid, MD

Photographs ©: Shutterstock Images, 5, 7, 11, 13, 20, 23,
24; Oleksii Natykach/Shutterstock Images, 6; Alila Sao
Mai/Shutterstock Images, 8, 9, 14, 19; Arvind Balaraman/
Shutterstock Images, 15; Sura Nualpradid/Shutterstock
Images, 17; Monkey Business Images/Shutterstock Images,
21

Front cover: Sebastian Kaulitzki/Shutterstock Images;
Shutterstock Images

ISBN: 978-1623235482
LCCN: 2013931356

Printed in the United States of America
Mankato, MN
July, 2013
PA02175

About the Author

Jane P. Gardner is a freelance science writer with a master's degree in Geology. She worked as a science teacher for several years before becoming a science writer. She has written textbooks, tests, laboratory experiments, and other books on biology, health, environmental science, chemistry, geography, Earth science, and math.

Table of Contents

CHAPTER 1
What Are Lungs?

Place your hand on your chest. Take a deep breath and hold it for a few seconds. Now let your breath out. Did you feel your chest rise a little bit? When you let the air out, your chest went back down. You just felt air moving in and out of your lungs.

You have two lungs inside your chest. The lungs are organs that are part of the **respiratory system**. The respiratory system is made up of the body parts that help us breathe. The lungs are behind the rib cage.

> Did you know you breathe in and out about 20,000 times a day?

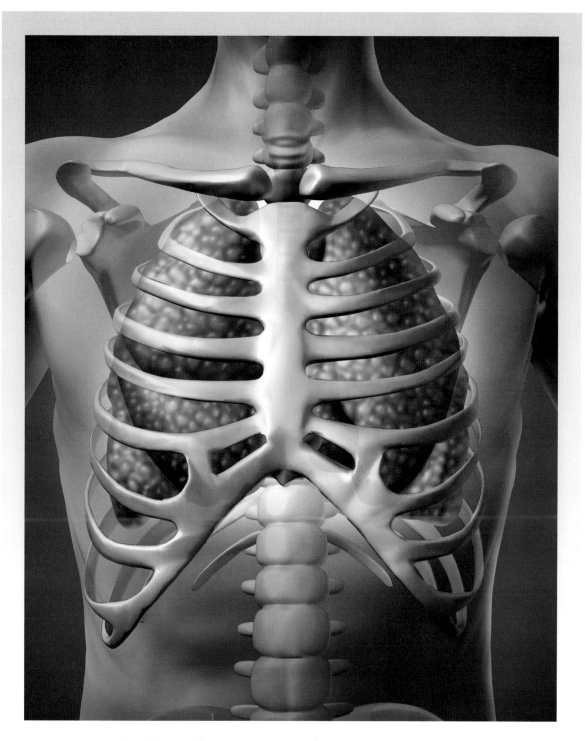

The rib bones form a cage around the lungs to protect them.

The left lung is smaller than the right lung. This is because the heart is on the left side of the chest. The left lung is smaller to make room for the heart. The left lung has two parts, or sections, called **lobes**. The right lung has three lobes.

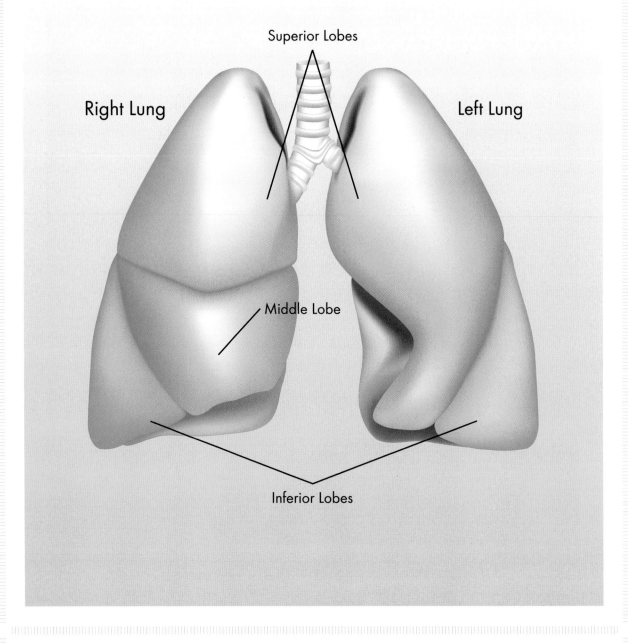

Superior Lobes

Right Lung

Left Lung

Middle Lobe

Inferior Lobes

These lobes act kind of like balloons every time you breathe in and out. The lobes fill with air and grow larger when you breathe in. Think of a time you blew up a balloon but did not tie it shut. When you let go, all of the air went out. The lobes go flat like a balloon when you let air out of your lungs.

Your lungs help you blow up a balloon.

CHAPTER 2

How We Breathe

The **diaphragm** is a very thin set of muscles just under your chest. When you breathe in, or **inhale**, the diaphragm moves down. This lets your lungs fill up with air.

Inhaling

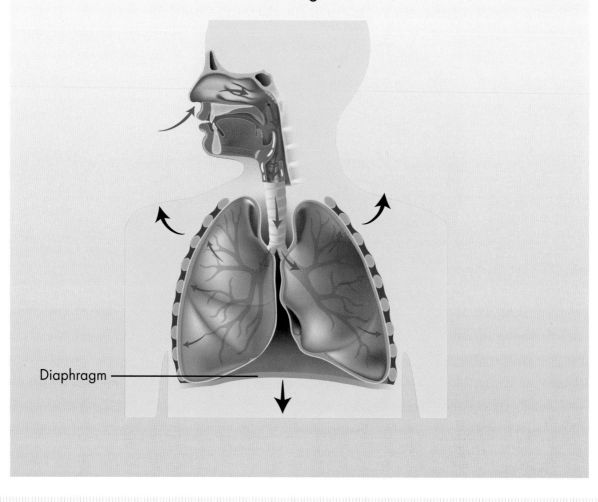

Diaphragm

When you breathe out, or **exhale**, the diaphragm relaxes. It moves up and pushes the air out of the lungs.

Hiccup! Sometimes your . . . hiccup! . . . diaphragm tightens in a funny way and makes you inhale too quickly. This can cause the hiccups.

Exhaling

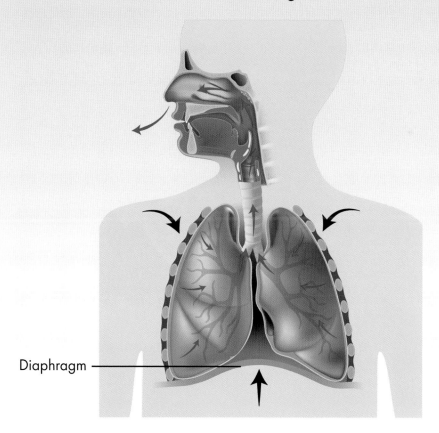

Diaphragm

You know that you use your lungs to breathe in air. But air is made of a lot of different gases. One of these gases is **oxygen**. All humans need oxygen to live.

Oxygen helps the body change food into energy. When this happens, another gas called **carbon dioxide** is made. Carbon dioxide is waste. Lungs carry carbon dioxide out of the body when you exhale.

When you get tired, your breathing slows down. Less oxygen comes into your lungs. Your brain tells your lungs to take a deeper breath, so you yawn.

Yawning is your brain's way of telling you to wake up.

Air enters the body through the nose and the mouth. Then the air moves down the windpipe. The windpipe is also called the **trachea**. The trachea is a tube that connects the throat to the lungs. The trachea splits into two different tubes called the right **bronchus** and the left bronchus.

Inside the lungs, the right bronchus and left bronchus split even more. They branch out into thousands of smaller tubes called **bronchioles**. At the very end of the bronchioles are small sacs. These sacs are called **alveoli**. When air comes into the lungs, the alveoli fill up like small, round balloons. When the air moves out of the lungs, the alveoli go flat. This happens every time you breathe in and out.

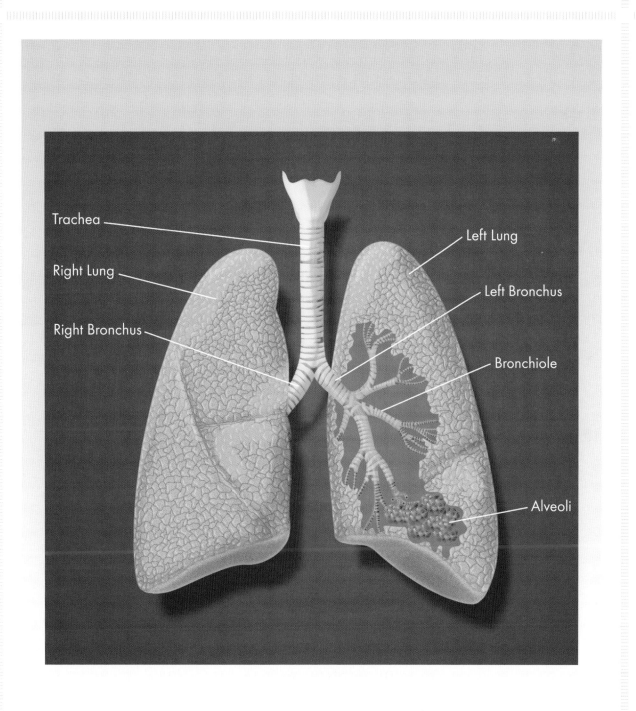

Trachea

Right Lung

Right Bronchus

Left Lung

Left Bronchus

Bronchiole

Alveoli

CHAPTER 3

Problems with the Lungs

Sometimes problems can happen inside the lungs. Asthma is a common disease of the lungs. About one out of every 12 people has asthma. During an asthma attack, the bronchioles tighten up and become smaller. This makes it hard for the person to get enough air to the lungs.

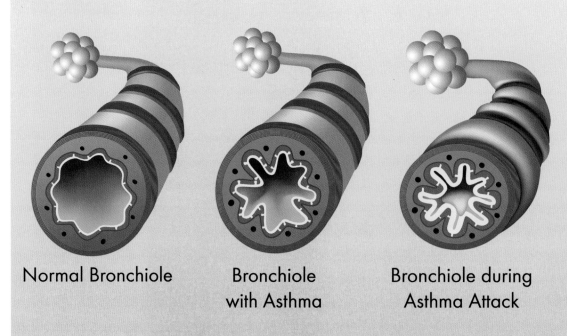

Normal Bronchiole   Bronchiole with Asthma   Bronchiole during Asthma Attack

Allergies and pollution are two things that can cause asthma. There is no cure for asthma. People with asthma use medication and inhalers to help. Inhalers bring medicine right to their lungs.

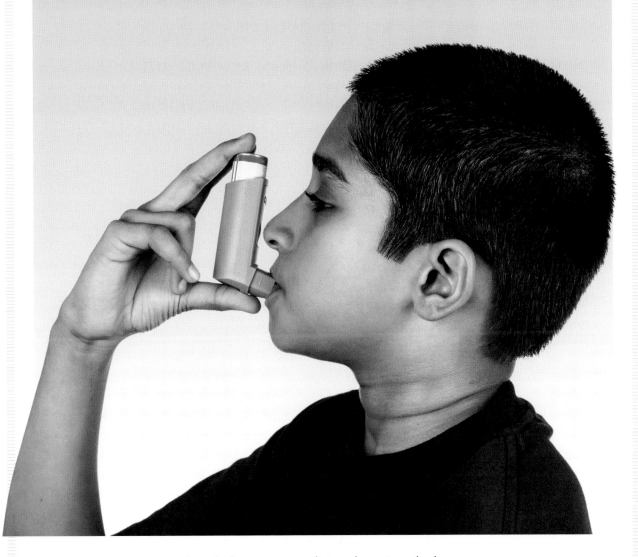

An inhaler sprays medicine down into the lungs.

Pneumonia is an infection that can happen in the lungs. During pneumonia, the lungs fill up with fluid. This makes it hard to breathe. A person with this infection may have a cough or a fever. People with pneumonia should rest and drink lots of fluids. They may need to take medicine. They may even need to go to the hospital. Pneumonia can be very dangerous.

Maybe you have had influenza. Influenza is also called the flu. The flu can sometimes damage the lungs and the whole respiratory system. The flu is a virus, and there are many different kinds. Influenza can be passed from one person to another.

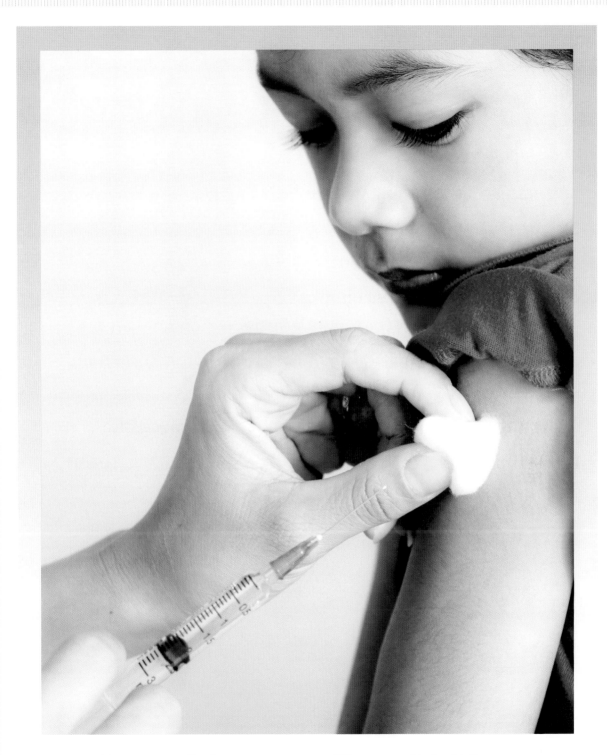

You can get a flu shot to protect yourself from some kinds of influenza.

CHAPTER 4
Breathe Healthy

It is important to keep your lungs healthy. Healthy lungs work better. They bring in more of the oxygen your body needs to live. You can help keep your lungs healthy.

Smoking damages the lungs. When a person smokes, the smoke that comes into the lungs leaves tar. Tar starts to build up on the lungs. This makes it hard for the lungs to get oxygen to the rest of the body. Inhaling secondhand smoke is also dangerous for the lungs. It is important to avoid inhaling any kind of smoke.

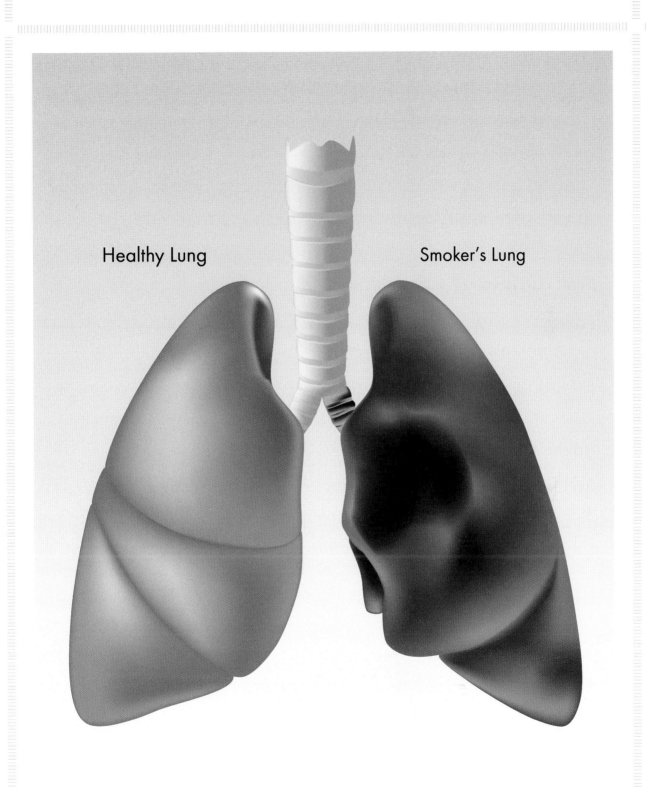

Healthy Lung

Smoker's Lung

Another way to protect your lungs is washing your hands. Washing your hands is a good way to avoid spreading germs and catching the flu. Be sure you get a flu shot. If you get sick, stay home from school. You don't want to pass the flu on to your friends. And the extra rest will help you feel better.

Wash your hands often to help stop the spread of germs.

You can also help keep your lungs in good shape by exercising. Think about what happens when you race your friend at recess. Your breathing gets heavy. You might sweat. You may need to gasp for air. These are all good things. This means your lungs are working hard to get more oxygen to your body.

You will start to breathe in deeper and bigger breaths of air the more you exercise. This makes your lungs stronger. It will help your lungs move oxygen to your body better, even when you are not exercising. Staying active keeps your body strong, and this includes keeping your lungs strong.

Running is great exercise for your body and lungs.

GLOSSARY

alveoli (al-VEE-oh-lye)
Alveoli are the small balloon-like sacs in the lungs. Gases are exchanged in the alveoli.

bronchioles (brahng-KEE-uhlz)
Bronchioles are smaller tubes that branch off of the right bronchus and left bronchus in the lungs. Alveoli are found at the end of the bronchioles.

bronchus (brahng-KUS)
The right bronchus and left bronchus are tubes that branch off of the trachea. They help bring air to the lungs.

carbon dioxide (KAHR-buhn dye-AHK-side)
Carbon dioxide is a gas found in the air. The lungs remove carbon dioxide from the body when you exhale.

diaphragm (DYE-uh-fram)
The diaphragm is the wall of muscle below the chest. The diaphragm helps pull air into your lungs and push it back out.

exhale (eks-HALE)
To exhale means to push air out of the lungs. Carbon dioxide is carried out of your body when you exhale.

inhale (in-HAYL)
To inhale means to bring air into the lungs. Oxygen is carried into your lungs and body when you inhale.

lobes (lohbz)
The lungs are divided into different sections called lobes. The left lung has two lobes, and the right lung has three.

oxygen (AHK-si-juhn)
Oxygen is a gas with no color in the air and water. Humans need oxygen to live.

respiratory system (RES-pur-uh-tor-ee sis-tuhm)
The respiratory system is the body system that supplies oxygen to the body and removes carbon dioxide. The nose, lungs, diaphragm, trachea, and right and left bronchus are all parts of the respiratory system.

trachea (tray-KEE-a)
The trachea is also called the windpipe. The trachea is the main tube air passes through to get to the lungs.

LEARN MORE

BOOKS

Burstein, John. *The Remarkable Respiratory System: How Do My Lungs Work?* New York: Crabtree, 2009.

Caster, Shannon. *Lungs*. New York: PowerKids Press, 2010.

Gray, Susan H. *The Lungs*. Chanhassen, MN: Child's World, 2006.

WEB SITES

Visit our Web site for links about the lungs: **childsworld.com/links**

Note to Parents, Teachers, and Librarians: We routinely verify our Web links to make sure they are safe and active sites. So encourage your readers to check them out!

INDEX